D1173865

Georgia, My State
Geographic Regions

Upper Coastal Plain

by Doraine Bennett

STATE STANDARDS PUBLISHING

Your State • Your Standards • Your Grade Level

Dear Educators, Librarians and Parents . . .

Thank you for choosing the *"Georgia, My State"* Series! We have designed this series to support the Georgia Department of Education's Georgia Performance Standards for elementary level Georgia studies. Each book in the series has been written at appropriate grade level as measured by the ATOS Readability Formula for Books (Accelerated Reader), the Lexile Framework for Reading, and the Fountas & Pinnell Benchmark Assessment System for Guided Reading. Photographs and/or illustrations, captions, and other design elements have been included to provide supportive visual messaging to enhance text comprehension. Glossary and Word Index sections introduce key new words and help young readers develop skills in locating and combining information.

We wish you all success in using the *"Georgia, My State"* Series to meet your student or child's learning needs. For additional sources of information, see www.georgiaencyclopedia.org.

Jill Ward, President

Publisher
State Standards Publishing, LLC
1788 Quail Hollow
Hamilton, GA 31811
USA
1.866.740.3056
www.statestandardspublishing.com

Library of Congress Cataloging-in-Publication Data
Bennett, Doraine, 1953-
  Upper Coastal Plain / by Doraine Bennett.
    p. cm. -- (Georgia, my state. Geographic Regions)
  Includes index.
  ISBN-13: 978-1-935077-21-3 (hardcover)
  ISBN-10: 1-935077-21-X (hardcover)
  ISBN-13: 978-1-935077-26-8 (pbk.
  ISBN-10: 1-935077-26-0 (pbk.)
  1. Georgia--Juvenile literature. 2. Georgia--Geography--Juvenile literature. I. Title.
  F286.3.B467 2009
  917.58'5--dc22
                          2009013004

Reprinted in the United States of America, North Mankato, Minnesota, July 2010, 070610.

2 3 4 5 6 — CG — 14 13 12 11 10

Table of Contents

The land is flatter in the Upper Coastal Plain. President Jimmy Carter lives here.

The Upper Coastal Plain is in south Georgia.

4

Let's Explore!

Hi, I'm Bagster. Let's explore the Upper Coastal Plain. It is Georgia's largest **geographic region**. A region is an area named for the way the land is formed. The **fall line** divides the Piedmont region from the Upper Coastal Plain. This is a strip of land that falls steeply.

Wiggle your toes in the sandy soil!

Rivers become wider in the Upper Coastal Plain. They move more slowly.

Wiggle Your Toes in the Soil

Land is flatter in the Upper Coastal Plain. A **plain** is a wide, flat area. Wiggle your toes in the soil. The ground is soft and sandy here. Rivers grow wider in the Upper Coastal Plain. They move more slowly. There are few rocks to make **rapids**. Rapids are fast moving waters in a river.

Scientists at the Coastal Plain Experiment Station help farmers. They study the best way to grow crops.

MY STATE

#11

Many crops are grown in rows, like these carrots.

Scientists Help Georgia Farmers

The summers are long and hot in the Upper Coastal Plain. Sometimes there is not enough rain. Scientists at the **Coastal Plain Experiment Station** help farmers. They study the best way to grow **row crops**. These are plants to eat that are grown in rows. Now, most of the row crops in Georgia are grown here.

Vidalia Onions are sold all over the world!

Peaches

Peanuts

Dairy Cows

Pecan Trees

Farmers grow many things in the Upper Coastal Plain.

Climb On the Tractor!

There are many farms in the Upper Coastal Plain. Farmers grow peanuts, peaches, and pecans. Cotton and carrots grow here. **Vidalia onions** grow here. They are sweet. They are sold all over the world! There are **dairy** farms, too. Farmers sell milk and cheese from cows and goats.

Jackie Robinson was born in the Upper Coastal Plain.

Appalachian Plateau

Blue Ridge

Valley and Ridge

Piedmont

Upper Coastal Plain

Lower Coastal Plain

Cairo, Georgia ★

Some blackwater rivers have white sand beaches!

Baseball and Blackwater

Jackie Robinson was born near Cairo, Georgia. He was the first African American to play major league baseball. Some rivers nearby are called **blackwater** rivers. The water in these rivers is clear and dark. But it's not dirty! Some have beaches made of beautiful white sand!

Pine trees are cut into lumber.

Lumber is used to build houses.

Farmers grow pine trees in the Upper Coastal Plain.

Pines Growing in Rows

Let's go farther south in the Upper Coastal Plain. The soil is very sandy here. It is too sandy to grow crops we can eat. Farmers here grow pine trees instead. You can't eat a pine tree! But you can build a house with pine **lumber**. These are boards made from trees when they are cut.

Providence Canyon was made by erosion.

Water causes erosion. It makes ditches in the soil.

Hike into Providence Canyon

Let's hike to the bottom of **Providence Canyon**. A canyon is a deep cut into the earth. It was made by **erosion**. Water washed the soil away. Rain ran off of land that was cleared for farming. The soil was not protected. The water made small ditches. The ditches grew larger and larger. Providence Canyon is still growing!

Scientists study the Kolomoki Mounds.

They found clay sculptures in the mounds.

The Creek Indians buried their chiefs in the Kolomoki Mounds.

Let's Visit Kolomoki Mounds

Creek Indians built the **Kolomoki Mounds** in this region. This is one of the largest Indian mounds in Georgia. The Indians buried their chiefs here. They also built temples on the mounds. Scientists found clay sculptures inside the mounds. Some sculptures looked like animals.

Riverboats like this once paddled up and down the rivers.

Motorboat

Jet ski

South Carolina

Savannah River

Chattahoochee River

Alabama

Upper Coastal Plain

Atlantic Ocean

Florida

Gulf of Mexico

Rivers in the Upper Coastal Plain separate Georgia from its neighbors.

Who is Next Door?

Georgia and Alabama are neighbors.

The **Chattahoochee River** separates

them. Georgia and South Carolina

are neighbors. The **Savannah River**

separates them. People once traveled

up and down the rivers on riverboats.

Today, we ride all kinds of boats. Even

jet skis!

Glossary

blackwater – A type of river in the Upper Coastal Plain that is clear and dark.

canyon – A deep cut into the earth.

Chattahoochee River – The river that separates Georgia from Alabama.

Coastal Plain Experiment Station – A place where scientists study the best way to grow crops in the sandy soil.

dairy – The milk and cheese that comes from cows and goats.

erosion – What happens to land when wind and water wash away the soil.

fall line – A steep strip of land that separates the Upper Coastal Plain from the Piedmont.

geographic region – An area named for the way the land is formed.

Kolomoki Mounds – An Indian burial ground and village site in the Upper Coastal Plain.

lumber – Boards made from pine trees that are used to build houses.

plain – A wide, flat area of land.

Providence Canyon – A canyon that was caused by rain running off the land.

rapids – Fast moving waters in rivers.

row crops – Plants to eat that are grown in rows by farmers.

Savannah River – The river that separates Georgia from South Carolina.

Vidalia onion – A special sweet onion that grows in the Upper Coastal Plain. They are sold all over the world.

Word Index

About the Author

Doraine Bennett has a degree in professional writing from Columbus State University in Columbus, Georgia, and has been writing and teaching writing for over twenty years. She has published 18 books for children, as well as magazine articles for both children and adults. She is the editor of the National Infantry Association's *Infantry Bugler* magazine. Doraine enjoys reading and flower gardening. She lives in Georgia with her husband, Cliff.